"In this small workbook, Heather Kendall has provided a simple, but clear and helpful introduction to what the Bible says about Satan and his work. Above all, as her chosen title has it, she rightly argues that Christ is greater than Satan. Once again, we see that in all things Christ has the pre-eminence."

—**DAVID H. J. GAY**

Director, David H. J. Gay Ministry, Bedfordshire, United Kingdom

"Satan is undoubtedly our Arch Enemy and one who we must not be ignorant of. Heather Kendall, in this Bible study, guides you in a comprehensive, orderly, and easy to follow outline that will be a rich blessing to you. She lays out all the key portions of Scripture that relate to Satan along with pertinent questions in each category that will help you to detect the wiles of the Devil, how to resist him, and the victory we can have; because 'greater is He that is in you, than he that is in the world.'"

—**GARY GEORGE**

Pastor, Sovereign Grace Chapel, Southbridge, Massachusetts

"I highly endorse Heather's new study, *One Greater Than Satan* . . . it gives another perspective on the story of redemption that will help people understand God's sovereign control of the circumstances of life and the place of sin and human responsibility. It is a good study for men and women, believer or unbeliever, for Christian growth or evangelism."

—**CLIFF LINNARD**

Pastor, Sovereign Grace Family Church, Belleville, Ontario

"Profitable Bible study sees Christ in all Scripture comprehensively and cohesively. Kendall's work has provided that overview for the seasoned believers and newest beginners in our Ladies' study. Applied to Satan's work, the focus on Christ in this study should prevent carelessness from taking the Accuser too lightly, and paralysis from fearing him too greatly, and thus prove equally useful to its readers."

—BRAD POWERS
Pastor of Berean Baptist Church, Sudbury, Ontario

"We have an enemy so stand guard. In the Christian life this is incredibly true and extraordinarily important. In *One Greater Than Satan*, author Heather Kendall not only helps us understand our enemy but gives necessary insight into how to stand our guard. This study will encourage and equip you as you grow in your faith in Jesus."

—DARREN JOHNSON
Lead Pastor, New Life Baptist Church, Innisfil, Ontario

One Greater Than Satan

One Greater Than Satan

A Christ-Centered Bible Study

HEATHER A. KENDALL

RESOURCE *Publications* · Eugene, Oregon

ONE GREATER THAN SATAN
A Christ-Centered Bible Study

Resource Publications
An Imprint of Wipf and Stock Publishers
199 W. 8th Ave., Suite 3
Eugene, OR 97401

www.wipfandstock.com

PAPERBACK ISBN: 978-1-5326-5369-8
HARDCOVER ISBN: 978-1-5326-5370-4
EBOOK ISBN: 978-1-5326-5371-1

Manufactured in the U.S.A.   09/20/18

Thank you to my husband for his encouragement, and to the ladies' Tuesday morning Bible study for their helpful input.

Contents

Introduction

> The Son is the radiance of God's glory and the exact representation of his being, sustaining all things by his powerful word. After he had provided purification for sins, he sat down at the right hand of the Majesty in heaven. So he became as much superior to the angels as the name he has inherited is superior to theirs (Heb 1:3, 4).

One Greater Than Satan, like *God's Unfolding Story of Salvation,* is a Bible study based on *A Tale of Two Kingdoms.* Its title emphasizes the truth that King Jesus reigns over all, including Satan.

The Bible describes Satan's character and activity many times. However, it only records his conversation three times: in the Garden of Eden, in heaven concerning Job, and in the temptation of Jesus. From a human perspective, believers have a problem difficult to understand. How exactly does Satan try to thwart God's plan of salvation? The Bible contains examples of people whom Satan used to promote his evil intentions. It also explains how Satan tries to trip up believers. The resulting conflict boils down to a battle of the wills: God's, Satan's, and ours.

Thus we need to keep the following Scriptures in mind as we progress through these lessons:

> When tempted, no one should say, "God is tempting me." For God cannot be tempted by evil, nor does he tempt anyone; but each person is tempted when they are dragged away by their own evil desire and enticed. Then, after desire has conceived, it gives birth to sin; and sin, when it is full-grown, gives birth to death (Jas 1:13–15).

Do not love the world or anything in the world. If anyone loves the world, love for the Father is not in them. For everything in the world—the lust of the flesh, the lust of the eyes, and the pride of life—comes not from the Father but from the world. The world and its desires pass away, but whoever does the will of God lives forever (1 John 2:15–17).

As for you, you were dead in your transgressions and sins, in which you used to live when you followed the ways of this world and of the ruler of the kingdom of the air, the spirit who is now at work in those who are disobedient. All of us also lived among them at one time, gratifying the cravings of our flesh and following its desires and thoughts. Like the rest, we were by nature deserving of wrath (Eph 2:1–3).

These verses help to explain two kinds of people: those who trust in God for salvation through Jesus alone and those who do not. Whether a believer or a nonbeliever, we all struggle to assert our wills at times. When our will conflicts with God's will, we are responsible for our sinful actions, not God. When true believers insist on their own way, they fall into Satan's traps, damage their witness for the Lord, and grieve the Holy Spirit. Meanwhile nonbelievers become unwitting accomplices of Satan. No matter what happens, the Lord Jesus remains sovereign over Satan.

Lesson 1

Who is Satan?

Read Gen 1:31—2:1

    1. How does God describe creation including Satan?

Read Heb 1:14

    2. Why did God create Satan and the other angels?

Read Ezek 28:14; Isa 14:12; Rev 12:9

    3. By what other names does God call Satan?

    4. Describe what happened to Satan and why by completing the chart.

Verses	What happened?	Why?
Ezek 28:12–17		

Isa 14:12–15		
Rev 12:7–9		

5. Describe the characteristics of Satan by completing the chart.

Verses	Characteristic
Eph 6:12	
Luke 20:36	
Eph 3:8–11	
1 Pet 1:10–12	
Gen 3:1	
Eph 6:11	
Eph 6:16	
1 Pet 5:8	

6. Summarize what you have learned about Satan from the above chart.

Read Heb 1:1–6

7. What facts do you learn about Jesus?

8. How do you know Jesus is superior to Satan?

9. What name did Jesus inherit?

10. How did he inherit that name?

REFLECTION: WHAT DO YOU THINK ABOUT SATAN? HOW DOES THIS KNOWLEDGE MAKE YOU FEEL?

SUMMARY

Some nonbelievers do not believe in the existence of Satan while others worship him. Satan rejoices over both of those attitudes. God describes everything that he created as very good, but no one can escape death. In addition, all the wickedness in this world points to the existence of a powerful, actively evil, being. The Bible calls this person, Satan or the Devil. Although Jesus created Satan as a mighty angel, to worship Satan insults the living God. Jesus also created Satan as a finite being who does not know the future. In contrast, the Lord Jesus, the sovereign Creator, knows the end from the beginning.

Lesson 2

Satan's Traps

1. What does Satan want us to do? Complete the chart.

Verses	Satan wants us to:
John 8:44	
2 Cor 4:4	
2 Cor 11:14, 15	
Eph 2:1, 2	
Eph 4:27	
1 Thess 3:5	
2 Tim 2:26	

Read Col 1:13, 14

2. What has God promised believers?

Read Eph 6:10–13

    3. What is the best defence against Satan?

Read Eph 6:14–17

    4. List the full armor of God.

    5. How will God's armor protect believers from Satan's evil schemes?

Armor	Verses	Explanation
Belt of truth	John 14:6	
Breastplate of righteousness	Rom 3:21, 22	
Gospel of peace	Rom 5:1, 2	
Shield of faith	Eph 2:8, 9	
Helmet of salvation	Acts 4:10–12	
Sword of the Spirit	Heb 4:12, 13	

Read Eph 6:18

    6. How do we access God's protection?

Read Jas 4:7–10; 1 Pet 5:6–9

    7. How may a believer resist the devil's advances?

Read Rom 8:26, 27, 31–34

    8. Who prays for believers?

Read John 12:27–32

    9. What happened as a result of Jesus' death on the cross?

REFLECTION: HAS THE ARMOR OF GOD PROTECTED YOU FROM SATAN'S TRAPS? WHEN?

SUMMARY

Satan desires to blind the eyes of nonbelievers so that they never understand and accept the wonderful salvation offered to sinners. In addition, he goes about like a roaring lion trying to entice believers to sin and ruin their testimony. Thankfully, Jesus conquered Satan on the cross. Therefore Jesus will surely protect his people from falling for Satan's evil tactics, especially if we ask for his help.

Lesson 3

Satan in the Garden of Eden

Read Rev 12:7–9
  1. Who is the serpent?

Read Gen 3:1
  2. How does God describe the serpent?

  3. Why did the serpent ask Eve that question?

Compare Gen 2:16, 17 with Gen 3:2, 3.
  4. What did Eve add to God's words?

Read Gen 3:4–6
  5. How did Satan tempt Eve?

6. Why did Eve eat the forbidden fruit?

7. Why did Adam eat the forbidden fruit?

Read Gen 3:7–10

8. What did Adam and Eve do as soon as they had eaten the fruit?

9. How did they feel about God?

Read Gen 3:11–13

10. Who did Adam blame?

11. Who did Eve blame?

Read Gen 3:14, 15

12. What was the serpent's punishment?

13. Who did God promise to send one day?

Read Gen 3:16–20

14. How did God punish Adam and Eve?

Read Gen 3:21–24

    15. Why did God shed the blood of an animal?

    16. Why did God drive Adam and Eve out of the garden?

Read Gen 5:5, 8, 11

    17. What happens to every person ever born?

Read Rom 3:10–18, 23

    18. Why do people suffer spiritual death?

Read Rom 5:12–14; Rev 20:14, 15

    19. Explain how the actions of Adam and Eve have affected all of us.

    20. What two kinds of death do nonbelievers suffer?

REFLECTION: WHY CAN SATAN DECEIVE PEOPLE SO EASILY?

SUMMARY

Because Adam and Eve yielded to the serpent's temptation to be like God, everyone feels those same desires from birth. We think we can be self-sufficient; we do not need or want anything to do with God. However, the Lord had a plan. Satan`s tactics did not surprise him. God could have allowed all of us to die in our sin and rebellion, but he did not. He promised one who would come and crush Satan—the promised seed.

Satan and his demons use the same technique on us today. They tempt us with their lies. Resist Satan by aligning your thoughts with the Word of God. "Finally, brothers and sisters, whatever is true, whatever is noble, whatever is right, whatever is pure, whatever is lovely, whatever is admirable—if anything is excellent or praiseworthy—think about such things" (Phil 4:8).

Lesson 4

Job under Attack

Read Job 1:1–8

    1. How did God praise Job?

    2. Why do you think God singled out Job to Satan?

Read Job 1:9–11

    3. How did Satan react to God's praise of Job?

Read Job 1:12

    4. What limitations did God put on Satan's evil plan?

Read Job 1:13–19

    5. How did Satan attack Job?

6. What agents did Satan use to carry out his attacks?

Read Job 1:20–22

7. How did Job react to those events?

Read Job 2:1–8

8. What did God allow Satan to do next?

Read Job 2:9, 10

9. What advice did Job's wife give him?

10. How did Job answer her?

When three of Job's friends heard about all his troubles, they decided to go and comfort him. As soon as they saw him, they cried out in shock at his appearance and sat down beside him. For one week, "no one said a word to him, because they saw how great his suffering was" (Job 2:13). Then Job broke the silence by lamenting his birth.

Let us consider what Job's friends thought about his plight.

Read Job 4:1–9

11. What did Eliphaz think of Job and his situation?

Read Job 4:17–21; 5:17, 18

12. What did Eliphaz imply?

Read Job 8:1–6, 20

13. According to Bildad, why did Job's children die and why was Job suffering?

Read Job 11:1–20

14. What did Zophar think about Job's situation?

Read Job 12:1–10; 16:1–5

15. How did Job answer his friends?

Read Job 32:1–5; 33:1–14; 34:5–12

16. Why was Elihu angry?

17. What point did Elihu make?

Read Job 38:1–7; 40:6–9

18. What did God teach Job?

Read Job 42:1–6

19. What truths did Job acknowledge?

Read Job 42:12–17

20. How did the Lord bless Job?

REFLECTION: HOW DOES SUFFERING SOMETIMES BRING US INTO A CLOSER RELATIONSHIP WITH GOD?

SUMMARY

According to his sovereign will, the Lord God created each one of us. This means he knows our thought-life whereas Satan does not. God knew Job loved him and would remain faithful to the end. In so doing, Job's suffering would bring glory to God. From Job's point of view, suffering taught him more about God. Likewise, suffering can teach us how God operates. When we continue to trust him through the pain, we also bring glory to God.

Lesson 5

Unwitting Accomplices of Satan

EVER SINCE THE GARDEN of Eden, Satan wanted to prevent God from sending the promised seed—the one who would crush Satan's head. Meanwhile Pharaoh and Athaliah each had their own wicked agenda. Nevertheless, in carrying out their evil plans, they unwittingly became Satan's accomplices. If either Pharaoh or Athaliah had succeeded in their plans, then Satan would also have accomplished his desire of thwarting God's plan of salvation. How often the Lord God has proven his sovereignty and power over Satan. God would send the promised seed, Jesus, at the proper time in history.

PHARAOH, THE NAME GIVEN TO ALL THE KINGS OF EGYPT

Many years before, because of famine in the land of Canaan, Jacob and his family had moved to Egypt. God, in his providence, had already established Joseph as second in command to Pharaoh so that Joseph could store food during the seven years of plenty and prepare for the seven years of famine. In this way God's chosen people would not starve to death. After that generation had died, however, a new Pharaoh came to power who did not remember Joseph.

Read Exod 1:8–10

    1. Why was Pharaoh afraid?

Read Exod 1:11–14

    2. What did Pharaoh decide to do to the Israelites?

Read Exod 1:15–16

    3. What instructions did Pharaoh give the midwives?

Read Exod 1:17–21

    4. Why did God bless the midwives?

Read Exod 1:22

    5. What did Pharaoh order his people to do?

But God would not allow this to happen.

Read Exod 2:1–10

    6. Who did God protect?

Read Exod 12:31–39

    7. How many Israelite men fled from Egypt?

God changed Jacob's name to Israel. He is the grandson of Abram, whom God later called Abraham.

Read Gen 15:1–6

    8. How many descendants did God promise Abram?

Read Gen 22:2, 13–18

    9.What did God promise Abraham? Why?

Read Acts 3:24–26

    10. Why did God overrule the plans of Pharaoh?

ATHALIAH

Although all of the kings of the northern kingdom of Israel were evil, King Ahab was the wickedest. Influenced by his wife Jezebel, Ahab had introduced Baal worship to Israel. Therefore God chose Jehu to destroy all the males in Ahab's family (2 Kgs 9:6–10). While Ahaziah, king of Judah, was visiting his uncle Joram, king of Israel, Jehu attacked and killed both of them. Ahaziah was a grandson of Ahab, and Joram was a son. Athaliah is Ahaziah's mother.

Read 2 Chron 22:10–12

    1. What did Athaliah think that she had done?

    2. Why did she want to kill the royal princes?

3. What did Ahaziah's sister Jehosheba do?

Read 2 Chron 23:1–3, 11

4. What did Jehoiada do?

Read 2 Chron 23:12, 13

5. How did Athaliah react?

Read 2 Chron 23:14, 15

6. What happened to Athaliah?

Read 2 Sam 7:12, 16

7. What did God promise King David?

8. Why did God overrule Athaliah's plans?

REFLECTION: NOTICE HOW THE LORD ALLOWED SATAN AND PEOPLE TO CARRY OUT THEIR EVIL PLANS. HE DID NOT, HOWEVER, ALLOW THEM TO SUCCEED.

SUMMARY

If Pharaoh had succeeded in wiping out the Israelites, then God would not have been able to keep his everlasting covenant with Abraham to send Jesus. "The promises were spoken to Abraham and to his seed. Scripture does not say 'and to seeds,' meaning many people, but 'and to your seed,' meaning one person, who is Christ" (Gal 3:16). Jesus lived a perfect life, died on the cross for rebellious sinners, and rose from the dead for their justification (Rom 4:25). This is the gospel. Those who repent of their rebellious ways and turn by faith to believe this gospel become God's children and the offspring promised to Abraham (Rom 4:16, 17).

Likewise, if Athaliah had killed all the royal line of David, then God would not have been able to keep his promise to David. When the angel Gabriel appeared to Mary, he said, "Do not be afraid, Mary; you have found favor with God. You will conceive and give birth to a son, and you are to call him Jesus. He will be great and will be called the Son of the Most High. The Lord God will give him the throne of his father David, and he will reign over Jacob's descendants forever; his kingdom will never end" (Luke 1:30–33).

Lesson 6

More Unwitting Accomplices of Satan

SENNACHERIB, KING OF ASSYRIA

When men built the Tower of Babel, they were disobeying God's instructions to Noah to populate the earth. As a result, the Lord confused their languages so that they would scatter everywhere. In the process they began to worship local gods and cemented the relationship between religion and the state.

Thus, when the Assyrians conquered a city, they also destroyed the local god. "Filled with pride, the kings of Assyria thought that they were unbeatable. After one city fell, they attacked another, then another, until entire countries were under their authority."[1] When Sennacherib laid siege to Jerusalem, Satan certainly rejoiced.

Read Isa 36:13–22

1. Why did Sennacherib think he had conquered so many other nations?

---

1. Kendall, *A Tale of Two Kingdoms*, 167.

Read Isa 37:1–4

2. Why was Hezekiah so upset?

Read Isa 37:5–7

3. What did the Lord say to Hezekiah through Isaiah?

Afterward Sennacherib received a report that the king of Cush was marching to fight against him. He tried to put pressure on Hezekiah in a letter. Sennacherib reminded Hezekiah of all the countries conquered by the Assyrians. Hezekiah immediately went to the temple with the letter and prayed.

Read Isa 37:14–20

4. On what facts did Hezekiah base his appeal to God?

Read Isa 37:33, 34

5. What did God promise Hezekiah?

Read Isa 37:36–38

6. What happened to the Assyrian army and to Sennacherib?

Read Isa 37:35

7. Why did God overrule Sennacherib?

HAMAN, A NOBLE IN THE COURT OF XERXES, KING OF PERSIA

Haman became proud when King Xerxes commanded all the other royal officials to bow down to him, but the Jew Mordecai refused. This angered Haman so much that only killing Mordecai did not appease him. He wanted to destroy all the Jews. Haman's evil desires coincided with Satan's.

Read Esther 3:8–11

1. What did King Xerxes order? Notice he did not question Haman's motives or even ask the name of the "dangerous" people.

Haman thought his evil plan could not fail because, according to Persian law, the king's edict could not be annulled. Yet God would overrule it through the bravery of Queen Esther.

At this point Haman did not know that Mordecai had raised his cousin Esther. Before she became queen, Mordecai had instructed her to keep her nationality a secret. Moreover King Xerxes did not know that his edict included his wife. Nevertheless, if Esther tried to speak to the king without his summoning her, she could die. For this reason, Esther asked all the Jews in the capital of Susa to fast with her for three days. Then she stood in the entrance of the king's hall.

Read Esther 5:1–5

2. What happened when Esther approached the king?

3. What did she ask Xerxes?

Read Esther 5:6–8

4. What did Esther promise Xerxes?

Read Esther 5:9–14

    5. What made Haman so happy?

    6. What did Haman's wife suggest?

That night, unable to sleep, Xerxes asked for the record of his reign.

Read Esther 6:1–11

    7. What did Xerxes find out?

    8. What advice did Haman give Xerxes?

    9. What did Xerxes order Haman to do?

Read Esther 6:12–14

    10. As soon as Haman's advisors and his wife found out what had happened, what did they warn Haman would happen? Why?

Read Esther 7:1–4

    11. What did Esther ask the king?

Read Esther 7:5–10

    12. What happened to Haman?

Xerxes granted the Jews a new edict to counteract the original edict.

Read Esther 8:11–13

13. What could the Jews do? Why?

Read Esther 3:5, 6; 9:24, 25; 4:1; 10:1–3

14. Contrast Haman and Mordecai. Why did they experience such different fates?

REFLECTION: HAVE YOU ASKED THE HOLY SPIRIT FOR GUIDANCE AND STRENGTH TO STAND FIRM IN THE BATTLE AGAINST EVIL?

SUMMARY

Although Satan deceives and tempts people to commit evil acts, he does not have the power to force anyone to oppose God. We are responsible for our own actions. At the same time, Satan did want to thwart God's plan to send the promised seed. He gladly used Sennacherib and Haman to attempt to accomplish his evil purposes.

Lesson 7

Jesus under Attack

THE BIRTH OF JESUS

The false prophet Balaam lived 1400 years before Christ in the east near the Euphrates River. Meanwhile the Israelites had reached the plains of Moab and had camped there by the Jordan River. Terrified of the large number of Israelites descending on his land, Balak, king of Moab, sent for Balaam. He asked Balaam three times to curse the Israelites. Instead of cursing them, Balaam blessed them. Afterward God made Balaam prophesy: "A star will come out of Jacob; a scepter will rise out of Israel" (Num 24:17).

Read Matt 2:1–3

    1. Why did the wise men travel to Jerusalem?

    2. How did Herod react to the request of the wise men?

Read Matt 2:4–8

    3. Where would Jesus be born?

4. Why did Herod care about the exact time of the star's appearance?

5. What did Herod ask the wise men to do?

Herod acted as if he wanted to worship the newborn king. Yet he did not go with the wise men to find Jesus. Only the foreign wise men cared enough to search for the King of the Jews. After they had worshiped him, God warned them in a dream not to return to Herod. The Lord would not allow Herod to harm his son.

Read Matt 2:13–18

6. How did God protect Jesus from Herod?

7. How did Herod feel when he realized the wise men were not going to report to him?

8. How did Herod try to kill Jesus?

THE TEMPTATION OF JESUS

As soon as John the Baptist had baptized Jesus, the Holy Spirit descended on him like a dove. Then God the Father spoke, "This is my Son, whom I love; with him I am well pleased" (Matt 3:17). Immediately the Holy Spirit led Jesus into the wilderness so that the devil could tempt him. Jesus did not eat for forty days and forty nights. Being fully human, he was hungry. Like us, Jesus had physical, emotional, and spiritual needs.

Read Matt 4:3, 4

    1. What did Satan ask Jesus to do?

    2. What human need was Satan attacking?

    3. Why was it wrong for Jesus to satisfy his hunger?

Read Matt 4:5–7

    4. What did Satan ask Jesus to do?

    5. What human need was Satan attacking?

    6. Why was it wrong for Jesus to throw himself off the highest point of the temple?

Read Matt 4:8–11

    7. What did Satan ask Jesus to do?

    8. What human need was Satan attacking?

9. Why was it wrong for Jesus to accept Satan's offer?

Read Heb 2:14–18

10. Why did God the Father allow Satan to tempt Jesus?

11. Since Jesus passed the test, what can he do for us?

12. Since Jesus passed the test, what can he do to Satan?

REFLECTION: THE LORD REWARDS THOSE WHO PERSEVERE AND KEEP THE FAITH THROUGH DIFFICULTIES.

SUMMARY

Satan always hoped he could stop God's plan of salvation. In the Old Testament he wanted to kill the ancestors of Jesus. When Satan realized God had chosen the nation of Israel, he tried to eliminate them. When he found out the promised seed would come from King David, Satan targeted that family.

After Jesus' birth, Satan tried his best to kill him by using the evil and treacherous Herod. When unsuccessful, Satan attacked again just before Jesus began his public ministry. This time Satan tempted Jesus to obey *him* instead of God. Surely that would foil God's plan. But Jesus remained faithful and obedient to God the Father.

Lesson 8

The Final Assault

ON JESUS' VISITS TO Jerusalem, he often spent time with his good friends Mary, Martha, and Lazarus in nearby Bethany. One day, Lazarus became sick and died. Both Mary and Martha chided Jesus for not showing up until Lazarus had laid in the tomb for four days. Nevertheless, soon after he arrived, Jesus ordered Lazarus to come out of the tomb. Bringing Lazarus back from the dead became the catalyst leading to Jesus' death.

Read John 11:47–53

    1. What did the Sanhedrin, the Jewish high council, decide to do? Why?

    2. What did Caiaphas prophesy about why Jesus would die?

Read John 12:1–8

    3. What upset Judas Iscariot?

    4. Why was he so upset?

Read John 12:9–11

    5. What happened after Jesus raised Lazarus from the dead?

    6. Who did the chief priests decide to kill?

Read Luke 22:1–6

    7. Why did Judas go to the chief priests?

    8. Why do you think Judas betrayed Jesus?

    9. Explain why you think Satan could enter into Judas.

    10. Why did Judas want to betray Jesus in secret?

Read Matt 26:17–25; John 13:18–30

    11. How did Jesus show he controlled the timing of his death?

Read Matt 26:36–38, 45–50

    12. How did Jesus show he controlled the timing of his arrest?

Read Matt 27:1–10; 2 Cor 7:9–11

    13. How do you explain Judas' remorse?

14. Explain the difference between Judas' remorse and true repentance.

Read Acts 1:15–20

15. How did Judas fulfill Scripture?

Read Luke 20:9–19

16. What is the main point of this parable?

Read 1 John 4:10; Rom 5:6–8

17. Why did Jesus die?

Read 1 Cor 2:6–12

18. Did Satan understand God's marvelous plan of salvation before the crucifixion of Jesus? Explain why.

Read Matt 25:41; Rev 20:10

19. What is Satan's final destiny?

REFLECTION: JESUS PROVED HIS
SOVEREIGNTY AND POWER IN DEALING
WITH LAZARUS, AND ALSO IN HIS DEATH,
RESURRECTION, AND ASCENSION. DO YOU
TRUST JESUS TO PROTECT YOU FROM YIELDING
TO SATAN WHEN HE ATTACKS AND TEMPTS
YOU?

SUMMARY

The teachers of the law and the chief priests desired to kill Jesus because they did not want to lose their power and influence over the
people. Likewise, Satan likely thought, "Let's kill Jesus and humans
will be under my control forever." That is why Satan used Judas and
the Jewish leaders to accomplish his own agenda. Little did Satan
realize that God had planned for Jesus to die, the righteous for the
unrighteous.

FINAL THOUGHTS

Have you accepted Jesus as your Lord and Savior? Do you believe
that the Lord God is sovereign over all creation? Do you accept
that, in the battle of the wills, God will always accomplish his purposes? If not, Satan will gladly target you to fall for his deceptions.

Believers know God defeated Satan at the cross, but we also
recognize that Satan remains active in this world. Nevertheless,
with Jesus and the Holy Spirit praying for us and watching over us,
what have we to fear from Satan?

> If God is for us, who can be against us? . . . Who shall
> separate us from the love of Christ? . . . For I am con-
> vinced that neither death nor life, neither angels nor
> demons, neither the present nor the future, nor any

powers, neither height nor depth, nor anything else in all creation, will be able to separate us from the love of God that is in Christ Jesus our Lord (Rom 8:31, 35, 38, 39).

Martin Luther expressed this truth in his hymn:

A mighty fortress is our God, A bulwark never failing;
Our helper He amid the flood Of mortal ills prevailing.
For still our ancient foe Doth seek to work us woe—
His craft and pow'r are great, And armed with cruel hate,
On earth is not his equal.

Did we in our own strength confide, Our striving would be losing,
Were not the right man on our side, The man of God's own choosing.
Dost ask who that may be? Christ Jesus, it is He—
Lord Sabaoth His name, From age to age the same,
And he must win the battle.

And tho this world, with devils filled, Should threaten to undo us,
We will not fear, for God hath willed His truth to triumph thru us.
The prince of darkness grim, We tremble not for him—
His rage we can endure, For lo, his doom is sure:
One little word shall fell him.

(Translated from the German by Frederick H. Hedge; based on Psalm 46.[1])

1. Luther, "A Mighty Fortress Is Our God," in *The Hymnal for Worship & Celebration*, 26.

Bibliography

Kendall, Heather A. *A Tale of Two Kingdoms*. Belleville, ON: Guardian, 2006.

Luther, Martin. "A Mighty Fortress Is Our God." In *The Hymnal for Worship & Celebration*. Waco, TX: Word Music, 1986.

www.ingramcontent.com/pod-product-compliance
Lightning Source LLC
Chambersburg PA
CBHW051049030426

42339CB00006B/267